13 YEARS FREELY A SLAVE

And My
Road to
Freedom
in Christ

BELLE LEE

WestBow
PRESS®
A DIVISION OF THOMAS NELSON
& ZONDERVAN

WestBow Press books may be ordered through booksellers or by contacting:

WestBow Press
A Division of Thomas Nelson & Zondervan
1663 Liberty Drive
Bloomington, IN 47403
www.westbowpress.com
1 (866) 928-1240

ISBN: 978-1-9736-2222-2 (sc)
ISBN: 978-1-9736-2221-5 (e)

Print information available on the last page.

WestBow Press rev. date: 3/7/2018

INTRODUCTION

What you are about to read is a look into my thirteen years as a previous victim of abuse. While I could write many stories on events that occurred during my time with Daniel, I did not want to bring light to all the traumatic events that occurred, I instead allowed God to lead me on which incidents to share with you in this book. *For protective reasons, names of people and places have been changed.*

You see, although I had many daily things happen to me, I overcame. I look back at the most difficult moments in those years and I can clearly see where God was in those circumstances. His word truthfully states, in this life we will have trials, but take heart, he has overcome! Nowhere does it say, we will have trials and go through them alone, so figure it out. He was there all along, and it is because of his Mercy and Grace, because of the overwhelming Love that Jesus has for us that I am here today, alive, stronger than ever, sharing my life as a Testimony, it is because of Jesus that I am no longer a victim, but I am now *VICTORIOUS*!

My hope is that as you read this, you will understand that no one is alone in their lives. We are called to carry one another. And in sharing my life with you, I am praying to be able to carry you out of what may seem like darkness into the beautiful light that is Jesus. My prayer is that as you read the words, God will speak clearly to you, in giving you direction, wisdom, clarity, and hope that will overflow from you into others that need it.

It may not be abuse you are, or have experienced, but we all have our trials we face in life. Don't let the lies set in telling you that your trial is not big enough to concern others with. I felt that way for many years, and that caused more isolation than I could have ever thought possible. Not one of us is meant to walk alone. In scripture, as Jesus was walking to his crucifixion, **MATTHEW 27:32 "ALONG THE WAY, THEY CAME ACROSS A MAN NAMED SIMON WHO WAS FROM CYRENE, AND THE SOLDIERS FORCED HIM TO CARRY JESUS' CROSS".** This wasn't a coincidence, just like those people who happen to cross your path at just the right time. No matter where you are at in your life right now, or where you end up tomorrow, just remember, in every situation, there is only one way out, one hope, his name is Jesus.

Many Blessings to you!

CHAPTER ONE
1987, WHEN IT ALL BEGAN

I remember the day like it was yesterday. My grandparents were at bingo, like they were almost every night of the week, and my sister was out with her friends, being three years older than me, it was a little easier to get out of the house since she had her own car. 15 years old, I was already considered a troublemaker, a runaway for the past couple of years, a liar, someone who skipped school, someone who would never amount to anything. So naturally when my best friend and her sister asked me if I wanted to sneak out and go to the club that was once named Starship, I went, even though we were underage. I had the perfect purple stonewash pants and I knew my grandmother had the perfect shirt to match, so of course I went into her room which was forbidden and got the purple striped shirt to match. And off we went.

The doorman knew my friend's sister, so he didn't question us. I had never been to a club before this. No matter how much trouble I got myself into, I really was a scared, careful girl. Although my family would never believe that. So here I was with music blaring, no idea how to even dance, drinking a coke and trying to look like I was a natural at this.

The first thing that caught my eye was a guy with a diamond tie looking right at me. Oh, I was flattered! He was very good looking, dressed in white slacks, a white jacket and that sparkling white diamond tie! My friend quickly takes my watch off and tells me to go over and ask him for the time. So off I go. He tells me the time, and I have nothing else to say so I just walk away. Well then, he stops me and asks me to dance to the next slow song because he wants to be able to be close to me to get to know me better. What?! A guy like this wants to talk to me? Wants to know me? I doubted that. Not if he knew my life story. But I smiled and said yes. So, the next song he comes up to me and immediately declares that the song was going to be our song. It was "Two Occasions". I wish I had known this was a sign, a warning, something to look out for. Had I known it was a form of controlling, a sign of abuse, but I had no way to know. I had no one to warn me of any of this. So, for me? It was all romantic and special.

This guy was really into me. While we danced he asked me about myself. I was not going to open with, "oh, I come from a family of physical abuse, sexual abuse, verbal abuse, incest, I was left with my grandparents as a baby, I am surrounded by alcoholism and negativity all the time, I only see my dad who lives miles away some summers…" that just did not seem like something that would win this guy over. So, I let him talk about himself, and said very little. Another mistake. I spent the rest of the night hanging out with him and what I thought was his roommate (I will get to that later in the book). He proceeded to tell me he had just broken up with a girl he was in love with. He said this as he was holding me and telling me how much he wanted us to get together from that point on. Yes, I was blinded by his attention and couldn't see beyond what I was feeling. It was around 1:45AM by the time we said our good-byes and I walked home.

Well, when I got home, the deadbolt was locked. When I knocked my grandmother came to the door and began cursing at me. She told me I needed to go back to the streets and stay there. She pulled me in as she began to beat me with the buckle of the belt I knew only too well on my back, as she cursed at me. I tried my best to block the beating but was unsuccessful. When she was too tired to continue, she told me to get out, so at 15 years old, there I was with only what I had on, no jacket, no money, no car, no family. Remember, cell phones were not around back then. So, I began to walk to my friend's house wishing I had just left with them at the club. They lived a couple of miles away and it was dark. I found a stick and kept going. Dog's barking, car's driving slow past me, but I made it safely close to 4:00AM. Her mom was way cool in my eye's back then, she let her kid's do what they wanted as long as they stayed out of trouble. So, when I showed up at the door she had no problem with me staying there, and she was not about to call the police or my grandparents. So, I stayed there for three nights, then I called the guy I had met at the club.

We will call him "Daniel". Daniel had told me he had a middle name he preferred which I found out later he did not actually have a middle name at all. I told Daniel what had happened, and he immediately suggested that I go stay with him and his roommate. He said it would be strictly as friends, that his family in California would send him money to help, and that he would use some to help me get a place.

He was working at McDonald's, but he said that was just to kill some time. He didn't have a car, so he rode his skateboard everywhere. He told me that even though he was nineteen years old, that he had to leave his car in California because his parents wanted to make sure he was going back. His Roommate never said any different, and Daniel seemed so genuine, so kind. He showed me his place, said he would help me get some of my stuff back so I could have clothes. This guy really cared. He explained that if I didn't stay there, I really had nowhere to go. That my family had already shown they didn't want me. That he would do everything he could to take care of me. So, I moved in. It seemed I was finally going to be safe. How easily manipulated I was!

JEREMIAH 9:4-6 NIV

"BEWARE OF YOUR NEIGHBOR!
DON'T EVEN TRUST YOUR BROTHER!
FOR BROTHER
TAKES ADVANTAGE
OF BROTHER,
AND FRIEND
SLANDERS FRIEND.
THEY ALL FOOL
AND DEFRAUD EACH OTHER;
NO ONE TELLS THE TRUTH.
WITH PRACTICED TONGUES
THEY TELL LIES;
THEY WEAR THEMSELVES OUT
WITH ALL THEIR SINNING.
THEY PILE LIE UPON LIE
AND UTTERLY REFUSE
TO ACKNOWLEDGE ME"
SAYS THE LORD

In this life, we all are looking for acceptance.
But what happens when that acceptance comes with a price?
God offers us full acceptance, love, forgiveness, compassion, grace,
and everything else each one of us needs and wants.
The best thing is, all that he offers! It is given in TRUTH.
Do not fall prey to the lies of man,
but fall into the arms of the one who will never fail you.

CHAPTER TWO
THE MOVE IN

That very night, he asked what the schedule of my family was. I told him my grandparents went to bingo religiously and whether I was there or not would not make a difference. So late that night we all took off to my grandparents' place, Daniel on his skateboard and me and his roommate walking. And as I figured, they were gone. So, first thing I tried to do was knock & check the door not knowing if my sister may be home. But no one was there.

I thought that would be it, but they were already taking off the screen to one of the windows and using some kind of tool to loosen the lock, so the window would open. I was so scared! After all, I knew the beatings I would get from my grandparents, but Daniel told me not to worry that they would never hurt me again. Once again, I felt so safe and protected. So, I did what he said and climbed in the window, went to grab some clothes, and my favorite stuffed animal, Kris Mutt. (Who would come in handy in the worst way later). And out of spite and hurt, I went into my grandparents' room and took a couple of shirts from there as well as a couple of pictures from a gray metal box we used to have that kept memories and important papers. I threw all this out to Daniel and then climbed back out.

We left the screen off, on purpose I think. Looking back, I see how much anger Daniel had, but I sure didn't see it then. So, carrying all this stuff which really wasn't much, we went back to his place, which would now become my home.

Daniel seemed to be such a gentleman, he let me sleep beside him, with Kris Mutt in the middle and didn't try anything, he taught me how to cook some meals because I knew nothing about cooking, he showed me how to clean, he even told me to quit my job at Burger King saying he would take care of me. Of course, this made sense to me because the money I was making there I had to give back to my grandparents when I lived at home, and now that I was with Daniel I didn't want to take the chance they may show up there and try to force me back home. I knew if I ever went back they would beat me even worse than the day I had left. It never occurred to me that now I would be able to keep that money. It would be the last job I would be allowed to have in my 13 years with Daniel.

After the first blissful first two weeks, things began to change. My role began to take place, but it was done so gracefully on his part that I did not even notice until it was too late. The first was him deciding that Kris Mutt needed to sleep on the other side of me, and I needed to be beside him so he could hold me. Before I knew it, he was having his way. I just laid as still as I could. I did not stop him. After all, this was a guy who was taking care of me, right? It was the least I could do. It wasn't like the time I had been raped. This was different, because surely if I had said no he would have stopped. Right? I would soon find out that no matter what I said, no meant nothing to him. When he would go to work I would have to gather the hem of his pants and pin them just the way he liked. Cook for him before he left and when he came back. Make sure the place was clean. Little did I know he was grooming me for what was to come.

The older sister of my friend that I went to the club with that night began to date Daniel's roommate. So, I felt that would help with where it seemed my relationship with Daniel was going. But we may have been living in separate worlds because Daniel made sure they kept their life apart from ours. Looking back, I can see why he wanted distance. When I would see his roommate and girlfriend together I could easily see how much he cared for her and how they were falling in love. I found myself quickly becoming jealous of what they had and confused as to why Daniel and I couldn't have that.

After being at the apartment for almost two months, Daniel told me that we were having to move to a small town outside of the city. He said that this was where his roommate's family lived and that his California family had sent a trailer for him to stay at there. I began to wonder about where all the money was that they were supposed to be sending, but he always had a very good reason about everything, so of course I believed him. How could I not? And I never pressed the question because I was already "trained" on what my place was, and what I was and wasn't allowed to do. He said once we were situated there that his family would send money and we would be able to get a home. I asked about his home in California, it sounded so beautiful! I could not wait to go see this place! So, as we prepared to move what little stuff we had, I was still feeling pretty optimistic about everything. After all, I knew this was only temporary and soon I would be living in California with this guy who loved me, which I was certain once we were surrounded with his family he wouldn't be as stressed and finally show me the love he felt for me. And on top of that, I would be a part of a family who was rich! How lucky was I! Boy, was I in for the biggest shock of my life.

JAMES 4:13-14 NIV

**LOOK HERE, YOU WHO SAY,
"TODAY OR TOMORROW
WE ARE GOING
TO A CERTAIN TOWN AND
WILL STAY THERE A YEAR.
WE WILL DO BUSINESS
THERE AND MAKE A PROFIT."
HOW DO YOU KNOW WHAT
YOUR LIFE WILL BE
LIKE TOMORROW?
YOUR LIFE IS LIKE THE
MORNING FOG-IT'S HERE
FOR A LITTLE WHILE,
THEN IT'S GONE.**

How many plans, dreams, goals do we make in life certain that it will all play out the way we visualize? We do this knowing in the past it has never worked that way, yet we continue to believe. What is it that we are putting our hope and faith in? There is nothing wrong with dreaming, having goals, but we must remember to always turn those over to God and allow him to unfold it all in a way that is best for us. For when we do it in our own will, we are only setting ourselves up for failure, hurt, and possible destruction.

CHAPTER THREE
MY NEW HOME

The sign said population 2,000. What was now my new home town. We had borrowed the car of the family we were going to be living with to move our stuff in. As we were driving into the town I was looking around for sights. Stores. Restaurants. Malls. Anything really. I was a girl who grew up most summers in a very populated big city, and the rest of the time in a city with a population of around 300,000. To not see anything when I looked around had me confused. Daniel told me that it was just temporary, so for me to quit looking so scared. He thought it was funny how shocked I was. I didn't want to appear as a little girl, although I was only 15, so I changed my attitude and tried to be cool about everything.

It took us no more than what seemed like three minutes from getting to town to driving up to the place that would become home. And I use that word very loosely here. I can still see every detail.

We drove up to what, in its best condition, would have reminded me of a broken-down kid's castle. It had a gravel driveway, there was a big porch in front with a couple of steps leading up to a wood door that looked like it had been kicked in a few times. The house was white and had two corner towers that resembled that of a castle. The house was cracking in various places and this was just what I could see driving up.

On the left of the house sat a small trailer, the kind you would attach to a hitch and pull around with you. I had seen some people use things like this when I would go fishing with my dad. This one was a very old looking one though and looked like it had not been used in ages. We had no more than turned off the car and all these girls came running out of the house. Some small and some older. One was carrying a little baby girl. They ran to Daniel's roommate and hugged him saying they had missed him, he immediately began introducing them to my friend. Then ran to Daniel calling him another name and trying to hug him but he was very stand-offish and never once tried to introduce me. I just smiled, and Daniel grabbed me and led me to the trailer that was off to the side. I just assumed he was going to show me around. I asked him who all those people had been, he told me they were his roommates family. Said they had been nice enough to let him stay until his family from California came for him. That he had been staying there just until he graduated high school. But for me not to talk to them. He didn't give me a reason, he just told me what to do and the subject was dropped.

We walked up to the trailer, it was locked from the outside, Daniel had a key that he must have had the entire time because I had never seen him get one at any point from any one person. At this point all the people that had been outside, including his roommate had all gone inside the white house. We stepped into what would become my new nightmare. There was a bed up on the right side that you had to climb to get onto with a stained sheet on it, and on the floor, was green carpet that was almost like a green turf texture, and off to the left was a little bench on either side to sit on. Directly to the left where I was standing there was a tall, narrow closet that had a lock on it. Directly in front was a small counter with what looked like used to once be a sink. And right up on the far-left side was a small window that was about the size of a notebook paper and was high up. That was the only light that came into the depressing look of this place. And all this was visible right from where I stood at the front door. This was the smallest place I can ever remember seeing. Even bathrooms I had been in seemed bigger than this.

I knew I must have looked stunned to Daniel. After taking everything in I looked at him only to see that he had been watching my reaction. I smiled and turned ready to get out of that place and into the white house, surely anything would be better than this. But he held my hand and kept me in place and pulled me in, closed the door, and began once more to have his way with me. This time I was in tears, but very silent. The thing is, Daniel saw my tears, and was in no way affected. He said for me to get comfortable in there, that he would be back later. I told him I didn't want to stay in there, trying not to sound whiny, but firm. He told me to quit complaining, that he was taking care of me. And with that he was out the door. Then I heard the most deafening sound. The same lock he took off was being placed back on the door and I heard the resounding 'click' as this guy who I thought loved me, this guy who I thought was going to take care of me, this guy who I had trusted was now locking me up like a dog in a crate just my size. With my hand on the door as if it would somehow melt away, I stood there and cried. My nightmare had just started.

PSALMS 10:10-11 NIV

**THEIR HELPLESS VICTIMS
ARE CRUSHED;
THEY FALL BENETH
THE STRENGTH OF
THE WICKED.
THE WICKED THINK,
"GOD ISN'T WATCHING US!
HE HAS CLOSED HIS EYES
AND WON'T EVEN SEE
WHAT WE DO!"**

So often it seems as if the ones who do not follow the path of God always come on top. It seems they have the wealth, the control, that they get away with most everything. Even Jesus was tempted by Satan with all the glory he would have if he just chose the way of him, and not the Lord, the selfish way. But Jesus was true to God. And in the same way we must be. It may seem like we are suffering at times, but keep your eyes upon the Lord, because he is watching over you, and over those who bring harm to you. When this life ends, we must all have to face eternal life in Christ, or in hell. In our Savior we can find hope, truth, faith, and a strength that will endure through all trials this world has. Take heart.... Jesus has overcome!

CHAPTER FOUR
CHAINED IN A TRAILER

I quickly adapted to my new life. I had no choice but to do so. I learned that no matter how much I cried, got angry, begged, tried to be sweet, nothing impacted Daniel's mind about what he was doing. He would bring me dinner from inside the white house, and lunch. Sometimes I would get breakfast. I was allowed out of the house to take a bath, which he would make absolutely certain that I did not talk with anyone during that time. There was a lady, which I assumed was his roommates mother, who would attempt to tell Daniel to let me sit down and eat. She would always try to get him to let me do things, but he always said no.

The first time I walked into the back part of the white house I was in just as much shock as when I saw the trailer. I could not see the entire house because Daniel took me in through the back door so that I could do what I was there for, nothing more, nothing less. What I did see, was a kitchen that was falling apart. Most of the cabinets did not have doors anymore. There was rust everywhere. The floor had tile in some places, other places there was nothing. The stove I found out had to be lit with matches each time anyone had to use it, and I had to use it every time I bathed. There was no hot water in the white house, so I had to heat water in pots on the stove then take it to the bath at least three times to at least get enough to have a decent bath. And I wasn't allowed a very long time. There were mice who would come scattering out from different places. But I embraced the few minutes I had outside the trailer.

I had nothing to occupy my time in the trailer. Daniel would leave for a couple of days at a time. I never knew when he would be coming back, or if he would. And no one would have known where I was. As the days passed, so did my desire for life. My hopes. My wishes, my wants and needs. I was quickly losing who I was. He would come back at times with panties and bras that he forced me to put on. Some were too small, others were too big, but he seemed to never notice. It made me sick to wear the stuff, to see the desire in his face when he looked at me, and more so to wonder where he got these items from. And it happened so often. The man that I had once admired began raping me nightly.

Remember the tall closet I mentioned in the beginning that had a lock on it? Well, because I had nothing to occupy my time with I started messing with the lock and because it was an old one it came off. To this day I wish it had never came off. Inside were pictures, lingerie, underclothes of all kinds that belonged to a woman and man whom I would find out later to some relatives. He would also tell me, either to scare me or brag, I would never know, that he would go to their place and peek through the windows to watch them and take pictures. I was living with a monster and I had no idea how to escape or where to escape to.

The days he was gone became longer and longer. There was no bathroom in the trailer. Most days I had nothing to eat or drink so going to the bathroom was not a problem. Well as the time went on I began to have to go to the bathroom a lot more and didn't know what I could do. I got my beloved Kris Mutt stuffed animal, and he became what I ended up having to use when I needed to go to the restroom. And when I had to, I would use a shirt to use for a bowel and wrapped it good, lift the benches and place them as far under as I could. Thank goodness that didn't happen very often.

After about what seemed like forever but was probably about 4 or 5 months of being in the trailer, Daniel came in very angry. He told me no matter what happened to stay inside. I became excited and scared. This meant he was not going to lock the door! Well he stormed out and within a few minutes I heard a lot of commotion outside the door. Someone was fighting! I was terrified now! I am not sure how long it lasted, but awhile later, one of the older girls came to the door, opened it and told me to come out. She was so nice, but I was so scared. I knew what could happen if I disobeyed Daniel. She told me not to worry, the she would talk with Daniel. I went to the back porch with her and sat down. She said it was time I knew the truth. I had no idea what she was talking about. I said okay, and just sat there afraid to say anything because I had no idea who she even was. I was just looking around for Daniel and expecting him to grab me and yank me back in the trailer. Until she said the next words, then she had my full attention. She told me that Daniel was her brother. That he had no family in California, that his roommate was his brother. That all of them were his family! She said he had always been ashamed of them and his life, so he would make up stories. That he had been lying to me. And even worse, that the ones fighting outside the trailer were Daniel, his brother (aka*roommate), and his father. That they fight all the time, only this time a rifle was involved. I am sitting there dumbfounded. Not only have I been living a nightmare, but I have been living it with someone I didn't even know! She apologized, and said she knew Daniel would be mad at her but that they felt I needed to know the truth. What in the world had I gotten myself into, and would I ever be able to get out?

PSALM 6:2-3;6-7 NIV

HAVE COMPASSION ON ME, LORD,
FOR I AM WEAK.
HEAL ME, LORD, FOR MY BONES
ARE IN AGONY.
I AM SICK AT HEART.
HOW LONG, O LORD,
UNTIL YOU RESTORE ME?
I AM WORN OUT
FROM SOBBING.
ALL NIGHT I FLOOD
MY BED FROM WEEPING,
DRENCHING IT WITH MY TEARS.
MY VISION IS BLURRED BY GRIEF;
MY EYES ARE WORN OUT
BECAUSE OF ALL
MY ENEMIES.

The feeling of loneliness can be so extreme at times. But loneliness does not mean the same as alone. You see, even when I was going through the most devastating times, I was not alone. God was right there holding me, just as he holds us all no matter what we face in life. We in the natural allow our emotions to overtake us at times and become so weary with life. But looking back at my life, I see every moment God was by my side. His word says that we will face trials in this world, but it never says we will do it alone. Allow him to get you through, and out of every mountain you may face. There is nothing too big, too ugly, too hard, too complicated for our God.

CHAPTER FIVE
I'M PREGNANT

I have no idea how long I sat there on the back porch, but eventually Daniel came over and looked right at, what I now knew to be his sister, with an angry look, then grabbed my arm to lift me up. She told him that I needed to know and that she wasn't sorry for telling me. I knew I was going to like this girl. For the little time I planned on staying anyway. I had no idea how I was going to get out, but I knew I had to somehow. I was living with a stranger, being forced to do horrible things!

Daniel lead me back into the trailer and told me he would be back. I grabbed his hand and said no, that I was not going to stay there. I let him know that I knew he had been lying to me and that I wanted him to take me back to my home city. He laughed as he began calling me names. He went on to telling me things that I now see were lies of the enemy. Speaking that no one would want me, and words that made me feel very worthless. I felt ugly by the end of all the hurtful words. All I could do was lay there and cry as he once again hurt me. As he walked out the last thing I remember hearing is the sound of the lock being placed on the chain.

I had been homeless before Daniel, I had been molested before Daniel, I had been raped before Daniel, I had been abused before Daniel, I had been abandoned before Daniel...but in all that, never had I felt so trapped as I did right at that moment.

Not certain how long I had been asleep, I woke to see the sun coming up. Another night Daniel had not come back. I was glad this time. I did not want to see him. If it meant I died in this trailer, so be it. I climbed up on the bench and looked out the little window as I had done many times to remind myself that there was life still outside of this four-wall confinement.

As I was standing there one of the other girls, another sister, came up to the window to get my attention. I was able to open the window a hair to speak with her. The other girls that were older came over. This would become a daily thing. They were so sweet to keep me company, they would do their best to try to pick the lock and get me out. It never did work. My life in the trailer became such a daily routine. With the exception of one thing. The clothes that Daniel was bringing began fitting tighter and I was having to pee a lot more. I had no idea what was going on, so I never said anything to Daniel. Not that he would care. He was just happy I was gaining weight. He said I looked like a skeleton on many occasions.

One night he actually decided to stay in the trailer with me, he had brought a whole new set of under clothes he wanted me to try on. I did as I was told. By this point I was so beat down I was losing all fight in me. I began to believe Daniel when he said I was worth nothing, that no one would want me. Well when I was on the process of changing, I left a trace of blood on one of the outfits. He immediately began to accuse me of being with someone, seriously? He kept me locked up, but somehow, I was having an affair! I was shell shocked at his outburst to say the least. I told him I didn't know what was wrong. But soon after I was throwing up. Now this had happened before, but I was able to lift the bench up and vomit under where I could cover the smell. But since Daniel was here I was not able to do this. Needless to say, he was disgusted and walked out. I sat there and cried not knowing what to do. I got dressed and threw all those nasty clothes onto a pile where I kept the stuff I didn't want to think about.

A few minutes passed, and I heard the door open, looking up I saw his sister. It had not registered that I didn't hear the lock. She told me to come inside, that it would be okay. I followed her in and for the first time was able to see the rest of the white house. It was falling apart. Everywhere you looked there was a fire hazard. How the house was standing, I had no idea. But I was so grateful to be out of the four-wall confinement that I would have been happy if the white house didn't even have a roof!

I went to the bathroom, washed up, then went to the sister's bedroom. Which was shared by all four sisters'. And not enough room for even two of them. They were all so sweet and of all ages. Well, the oldest helped me figure out what the bleeding, peeing, and vomiting was all about. I guess somewhere in me I knew, I just did not want it to be so. But for confirmation, Daniel actually took me to the city I grew up in which was only about one hour away, the next day to the clinic which we were told was a place based of income. They did a test on me and told us what I did not want to hear. They said I was pregnant. I had always wanted to be a mom, have a family, this was just not the way I pictured it going. Or the kind of man I pictured it with. But ready or not, we were about to become parents. I couldn't help but secretly hope that this baby would be what would change Daniel. That he would realize he was going to have a family and everything would be just as it was supposed to be. It could happen, right? Wrong. Very wrong.

JEREMIAH 8:4-6 NIV

JEREMIAH, SAY TO THE PEOPLE,
'THIS IS WHAT THE LORD SAYS:
"WHEN PEOPLE FALL DOWN,
DON'T THEY GET UP AGAIN?
WHEN THEY DISCOVER THEY'RE ON THE
WRONG ROAD, DON'T THEY TURN BACK?
THEN WHY DO THESE PEOPLE STAY ON THEIR
SELF-DESTRUCTIVE PATH? WHY DO THE
PEOPLE OF JERUSALEM REFUSE TO
TURN BACK? THEY CLING TO THEIR LIES
AND WILL NOT TURN AROUND. I LISTEN
TO THEIR CONVERSATIONS AND DON'T HEAR
A WORD OF TRUTH. IS ANYONE SORRY FOR DOING
WORNG? DOES ANYONE SAY, "WHAT A TERRIBLE
THING I HAVE DONE"? NO! ALL ARE RUNNING DOWN
THE PATH OF SIN AS SWIFTLY AS A HORSE
GALLOPING INTO BATTLE!

How easily we hold to our own flesh wants! We have all been guilty of knowing something is wrong, a decision, a choice, a path we take, the list goes on and on. Yet, in knowing it is self-destructing, or hurtful, or a lie from the enemy, we continue to convince ourselves that maybe, just maybe this time something will be different. Well friends, let me tell you, when God say's no, that means stay away! If we will just let go and allow God to guide us down his path, not the one we chose, but the one he has then we can let go of worry, hurt, fear, and control. Yes, we will still have difficulties, but the road itself will be less bumpy, less mountainous, and those waters will part like never before.

CHAPTER SIX

SEARCHING FOR ESCAPE

Here I was thinking things would finally be looking up with a baby on the way. I was now scheduled to go to regular appointments, but things weren't looking too good. I was still bleeding and not gaining much weight. I was now going on three months. I was however very thankful that I no longer was having to stay full time in the four-wall confinement trailer. Although there were times that Daniel would have his family lock me out of the white house, so I was forced to go back into the trailer and wait. Not eating for days at times. Ever since the truth had come out Daniel seemed to not care as much but at the same time seemed to be angrier. He had begun drinking, or at least I had just began seeing him drink. This really bothered me, but I was so happy about my new baby that I tried not to think about that.

Daniel had arranged a job doing some field work hoeing for the summertime. I had never done anything like this and was surprised when Daniel said I would be going to help. We were having to wake at 4:00AM to start work and worked until roughly 6:00PM or 7:00PM every day. The temperature would reach a high of around 95 to 100 degrees daily and we had to wear long sleeve shirts as to not get burned. His sisters and brother went with us as well and would always check on me, making sure I was drinking water. There was no bathroom, which I was used to being in the trailer, but the more pregnant I became, the more difficult it was to hold it in. I was nearing four months, still bleeding, and was getting miserable being in the heat. Daniel's mother was also pregnant. One month further along, which I was a little weirded by with her being so much older. But she kept telling me I would be fine because she was. Well she wasn't having to deal with what I was either! And she was able to take care of herself, unlike me. About this time, I was beginning to miss my family. I began to wonder if my mother would respond to my call if I could just find a way to call her. We had such a hit and miss relationship that I never knew if she would talk to me. But I was feeling I needed a way out for my baby's sake. I was getting desperate.

Back at the white house one afternoon, Daniel was busy working on a car with his dad and his mom was cooking, everyone seemed to be busy. I looked around and realized for the first time I was alone. Now was my chance. Terrified, I slowly walked to the girls' room where I could look out the window where Daniel was and grabbed the phone. I called my mother and prayed that she would, one, be home, two, answer, three, not hang up on me.

She answered. I began to cry, and told her I was scared, pregnant and needed her to come save me. To PLEASE come save me. She said she would be there for me. Said she loved me and had been so worried about me. I quickly told her where I was and said I had to hang up. This is one of the times I will forever be grateful that my mom put aside our differences to drop everything and come rescue me.

I hung up with my heart feeling like it was in my hand it was so loud. I was so glad Daniel stayed outside for as long as he did because I know my eyes must have been huge from fear and my body shaking from nerves. One of the sisters came in, the one I was getting closest to, and asked what was wrong. I confided in her and let her know what I did. For some reason I felt I could trust her. Even though Daniel was her brother, I believe she knew what he was doing, the way he was treating me, and our unborn baby was wrong. And I was right to be able to trust her. She quickly put the phone in the other room so Daniel wouldn't even suspect anything. She brought me a towel and said she was glad I had called.

I went back to get the laundry I had to wash and to the bathroom to wash it. There was no washer, or dryer. The way I had to wash clothes was on an old-time washboard in the bathtub with water that I heated on the stove top, then hang it up to dry on the clothesline outside. Sometimes I could almost believe I was in a little house on the prairie episode, only they were happy. No one was raped, locked up, starved, abused, or treated in all the other ways I had endured. But if I closed my eyes sometimes.... I could just pretend, at least until I was rescued. Soon, soon I knew my mom would be there. Then my baby would have a life. Then we would be okay.

When Daniel came in I had to make certain to hurry and take his food to him. I had been "trained" to cook for him (his mother was teaching me how to cook), and to serve him. I never thought I would be serving a man this way, but it seemed I had no choice. When he was thirsty, it was my job to jump up and get him drink. I had everything ready for him and sat beside him until I made sure he was okay, then I was able to go get some food to eat. Having been able to spend more time in the white house I had been able to watch more closely the family unit and I now understood why Daniel was the way he was. The saying that the apple doesn't fall far from the tree is what came to mind. It seemed to be a repeated pattern. It was no wonder Daniel had picked up bad habits. I could not wait to get out of this nightmare and have my life back. As messed up as it was, this was far worse than any messed up in my family.

By the end of dinner, a car was pulling up on the gravel. My heart began beating very fast and I was scared as ever! Daniel was the first to look outside and said it was two women that he did not recognize. His dad said in some foul language to tell them to go away. I knew my mom, she had been in some rough fights, she would not back down easy. If it was her. Daniel stayed at the door and all I heard was two doors close, then footsteps, and then the best sound ever, the voice of my mom. I was finally going to be free!

PSALMS 139:13-16 NIV

YOU MADE ALL THE DELICATE, INNER
PARTS OF MY BODY AND KNIT ME
TOGETHER IN MY MOTHER'S WOMB.
THANK YOU FOR MAKING ME SO
WONDERFULLY COMPEX! YOUR WORKMANSHIP
IS MARVELOUS -HOW WELL I KNOW IT.
YOU WATCHED ME AS I WAS BEING
FORMED IN UTTER SECLUSION, AS
I WAS WOVEN TOGETHER IN THE DARK
OF THE WOMB. YOU SAW ME BEFORE I WAS
BORN. EVERY DAY OF MY LIFE WAS
RECORDED IN YOUR BOOK. EVERY
MOMENT WAS LAID OUT
BEFORE A SINGLE DAY HAD PASSED.

Have you ever just wished you would have never been born? If we are being honest; the answer would be yes. Hurt can make us feel this, anger, betrayal, resentment, depression, etc. But as Christians, we have to remember in our most darkest times, it is vital that we recall God's promise on our life. HE KNEW US BEFORE WE WERE BORN! He has a grand plan for you, for me, for your neighbor, and yes, for that person you just don't really like. We are all called for a grander purpose. And while it may be hard to see in the darkness, when we focus on the light, you can see just that much better. During my 13 years I could not imagine I would be doing an inch of what God has me doing now. But Glory to God, I am loving and living it all! It may take a few years to see your purpose unfold, it may take one day, but however long it is, stay focused and remember, you were formed, woven, created, knit perfectly together for a purpose!

CHAPTER SEVEN
TURN OF EVENTS

Once my mother made it to the door, announced who she was, Daniel let her in, asking her how she knew I was there. She ignored him and came right up to me. I just hugged her & held on feeling like a little kid. She came and sat on the bed with me as I told her I was pregnant, trying to look as excited as possible. Daniel was not quick to leave my side. She said she was taking me home with her. Daniel's mom told him that he needed to go with me, but my mom said that whether he went or not that she was going to take me because I needed to get medical care for the baby. I felt like such a little kid sitting back watching our mom's talking for us and me just holding my breath wanting nothing more than to be taken out from this place. Finally, after what seemed like forever, an agreement was made to allow me to leave so I could get the care I needed. I took my mom to the trailer where I had the little bit of clothes I owned and the shock on her face made me look at it all over again. I felt dead inside at knowing this was what my life had come to. She asked me questions, shocked and angry that I had been living in the conditions that she was seeing. She asked if I had everything, I looked back and saw Kris Mutt, sadly with my head lowered, I said that was it and walked out.

On the drive to my mother's back in the city, I was asked question after question about how I had been surviving. Not living but surviving. My Mother looked at me with such a look of heartbreak in her eyes. I felt like a little girl curled up in the backseat. Yes, I was still just a little girl in age, but after what all I had been through, I was anything but little. Once we reached her place, she was quick to want to feed me, get me all comfortable in bed, and have me rest.

As I lay there trying to sleep, my mind wondered in trying so hard to try to feel "normal", yet I had no idea what that was like. I wanted to cry from the feeling of being free, I wanted to cry from missing Daniel and being mad from missing him, I wanted to cry for the little baby I was carrying, I wanted to cry because I just didn't know who I was anymore! But nothing came out. I could not cry. I lay there just feeling lost. Empty. Alone. Embarrassed. Ashamed. Thinking, now what?

Early the next morning we went to the Doctor, I was weighed, and my stomach was measured.

I was given some orange stuff to drink, they did some test with a machine that I later learned was called an ultrasound. It turned out that I was at high risk of losing the baby. She (I was told I was having a girl) would either be born early, or there was a high chance that either myself or baby would not survive. I was also told that this would be the only baby I would be able to have because of the risk involved. I was then placed on bed rest for the remainder of the pregnancy at just four and a half months.

Daniel called later that day and I filled him in on what the Doctor had said, he blamed me and said that if I had been faithful then I would not have contracted anything, I told him I was locked up, how could I do anything? But it was pointless. We argued, my voice was never heard, I cried, he won, I felt more defeated, and he gained more control. I would not tell my mom what he would say, but I always had a feeling she knew. There were times she would start to say something, and I would find myself defending him. And I never understood my own reasoning.

Later that day my grandmother and mother took me to the store to go and buy clothes to wear since I had nothing but the clothes that I had ran away with. I was at the point of wearing my jeans unzipped since they no longer fit. I was starting to feel spoiled with the attention I was getting of clothes shopping and going to eat. Needless to say, my fear of getting beat upon returning home ceased as I began to see how much my mother and grandmother were willing to do for my unborn baby. Then once home I was made to sit and have my feet up covered and not move for much of anything. My mother took such good care of me. For once I was not getting beat, called names, degraded, shamed or mistreated in any form. At least for the moment. That didn't last long.

I was at my mothers for a few day's getting into a routine of taking care of myself for the baby, enjoying the love I was receiving, finally feeling somewhat human even when I did have to talk to Daniel when he would call. But when he showed up at my mom's apartment, I was shocked, my mother was not happy to say the least. He was there with his bags, ready to move in. It was then that not only my world began to change, but my baby's world was about to also.

My mother did all she could to accommodate him, us, despite her own feelings. She knew by this time that if she didn't he would take me away. And why I had no fight in me, to this day I cannot answer that. Other than to say that in an abusive situation, a man will degrade a woman to the point she can no longer think for herself, all she thinks is what he thinks. And fear sets in. It is a horrible way to live, one no one should ever have to go through.

Daniel continuously wanted me to make him meals, wash his clothes, fix his pants, do the wife things for him. I was fine with that, but my mother let him know I was not to do any of this. He in turn let me know how useless I was. I was not able to be intimate with him during my pregnancy either, this was not something he was pleased with either. And I never heard the end of that. As a matter of fact, that is when my nightmare fully unfolded.

PSALMS 32:7-8 NIV

FOR YOU ARE MY HIDING PLACE; YOU PROTECT ME FROM TROUBLE. YOU SURROUND ME WITH SONGS OF VICTORY. THE LORD SAYS "I WILL GUIDE YOU ALONG THE BEST PATHWAY FOR YOUR LIFE. I WILL ADVISE YOU AND WATCH OVER YOU".

You know those times you feel like you are at that fork in the road and you stand there not certain which way you should go? Eventually you must have to choose, and so many times that choice leads us down a path God never intended us to walk down, but that does not mean he abandons us and leaves us to find our way back. If you find that you are walking down that road that you wish you had not taken, stop where you are and simply ask Jesus to guide you back to his plan and purpose for your life. Ask forgiveness for not seeking direction before. Our heavenly father lovingly awaits to take your hand and walk with you back into your promise land.

CHAPTER EIGHT
THE MOMENT OF TRUTH

Living with my mother didn't last too long. Soon our baby girl was born, and we were approved to move into a duplex apartment that was funded through the housing project based off our income where we lived. Daniel was working at a restaurant and had just started working as a security guard for a company that sent him to guard various places. Once we were in our own place things began to get even harder for me. I was made to keep all the blinds closed, the door was to not be opened, nor were my daughter and I to go outside. He claimed this was to keep us safe. I tried to tell myself it was ok, that it was only because he cared about us. But having been a child who was always outside, it was really difficult to be what I considered trapped inside.

When I first started complaining the verbal abuse started getting really bad. I was called everything from stupid, ugly, to derogatory names that I won't write. When he would leave for work I felt I could breath. My daughter and I had fun, until I knew he was about to come home I had to make sure everything was spotless, dinner had to be on the table, everything had to be in perfect condition when he walked in that door. I always felt more and more degraded when he would come home. He had a routine of checking everything he could trying to catch me doing something wrong. It had become a daily process. I would get my hopes up when I would see him play with the baby, but my hopes quickly diminished when he would go out to the car to get his alcohol. That also became a daily routine. Since I did not have a car, nor was I allowed to go out of the house I had two choices, trust in all that Daniel was doing, or let my mind wonder what all he did when he was gone. I chose to trust. I soon found out how naïve I was to have believed all he said at face value. I suppose somewhere in me I knew better, I just had always wanted to see the best in everyone. Even someone who treated me as horribly as he did. By this time, he had me dressing the way he wanted me to. I wore baggy pants, long shirts that had to cover my bottom half completely, and I could not wear certain makeup because in his words, I looked like a clown.

I thought I was doing everything possible to make him happy so there was no reason for him to complain or want anything else.

Well, on a night that he had worked double shifts of security (he had quit at the restaurant by this point) he had come home already drunk and continued to drink more when he was home until he passed out on the bed. It had been another night of him breaking beer bottles, calling me names, and raping me. I was always so thankful that God protected my baby and allowed her to sleep in her room, never waking to have to see this, at least not as a baby. I knew he would be out for a good while.

Looking back now, I think it was anger, hurt and frustration, but at the time I thought it was bravery. I made the decision to go through his wallet, car and work case that he carried around. My heart was beating so fast, even though I knew he was not going to wake up, I was so fearful this would be the one time he would wake up. Going through the car first I found what I recognized as a joint which was a shock to me. I had no clue he was doing drugs. I had only ever seen one person do a drug, so I wasn't familiar with the effects, especially mixed with alcohol. But not much else was in the car, or his work bag, but then when I went to his clothes where his wallet was, there was a small black book rubber banded together. Of course, guys in school always teased of having a black book, but that was for single guys. Daniel was not single! So why the black book? I sat in the living room staring at it for what seemed like hours but I'm certain was only minutes. Finally opening it my heart was crushed. I saw many initials with numbers beside them. Some of the initials had stars beside them, some had hearts, some had asterisks. Then he had the names of his coworkers, bosses, male friends, all with their full name. So as young as I was, as naïve, and as much as I tried to convince myself that our relationship was normal, I knew without a doubt that the initials were all females' numbers. I didn't know what I was going to do about it, but I had to do something. So, I copied all the phone numbers down and hid them in the kitchen under the cans of food where I knew Daniel wouldn't find them. Then I did all I could at that moment. I went to bed and cried myself to sleep.

The next morning was on a Saturday and I knew Daniel didn't work until the night time, so he would probably be sleeping in late. I went about all I was supposed to do, and spent time with my baby playing, bathing her, then laid her for a nap just about the time I heard Daniel moving around. I had so much fear inside at the thought of facing him, but I also had so much anger that it was snuffing out the fear. I went to the kitchen, made his breakfast, got everything situated for him like the good girlfriend I was supposed to be. I had to sit across from him when he was eating just in case he needed something, I had to be ready to grab what he needed or refill his drink before it was empty unless he said otherwise. He sat there and talked about work, his family, and himself for a while before finally realizing I wasn't saying anything.

He asked what my problem was, and all I could do was cry and get up, grab his black book and throw it at him. After calling me a few choice words and grabbing my hair so I could pick it up he asked why I had been going through his things, that I was never to touch any of his stuff. That hurt me even more thinking here he was making me feel like I was the one who had done something wrong when in fact it was him who had done the wrong! But he was good, he knew just how to twist things. However, even though I was feeling guilty I wasn't going to give in. I asked who all those girls in the book were. He told me they were all guys from work and clients that he met at work that wanted him to do security for them. I asked about the initials and was told it was faster than writing the names of all of them. I told him to call one of them on his phone if that was true. I guess I pushed it a little too much because after I said that he came after me and while calling me very crude names began to force himself on me, all the while accusing me of being the one cheating on him. He made me repeat disturbing things back to him that I in no way meant but knew I had to say. All the while I was still thinking, wondering what I was going to do next, knowing he was lying. My last thought at the end of that horrible night was, I will just have to call those numbers myself from the payphone down the street. As soon as I figured out how to get money for the phone.

From that day on, Daniel locked things up in the trunk of the car thinking I would never be around there. And the next time I looked in the black book which was a few days later, the initial list and numbers had grown longer.

I finally had enough change to make some phones calls, so when I knew Daniel was going to be gone overnight with work, I waited for just a bit when he left, got my baby in her stroller and headed to the phone. I'll never forget the first number I dialed, T.J were the initials. Once, twice, third ring some female answers. I ask for Daniel. She asked who this was, and I told her it was his wife and that he also had a baby and that she needed to stay away from him. She said that it wasn't her fault that I didn't knew how to keep a man. That Daniel went to her, she didn't go to him. I was shaking when I hung up. I called three more numbers that day, and all three of them confirmed Daniel was sleeping with them. I went home, cried and cried. I didn't know where I went wrong in my marriage, but I knew I didn't deserve this. But I loved him. I had his baby. Didn't that count for something? I had never been so torn on what to do. Who were these girls? Did he love them? Maybe they were lying to me. Maybe it was their husband Daniel knew. I decided I wouldn't say anything until I figured out what I was going to do. But it turned out that I didn't have to say anything. Daniel came home early that day, just for one reason only. To ask what business did I have calling T.J for anything. Having his hand around my throat and the anger in his eyes, I was speechless.

COLOSSIANS 3:13 NIV

"MAKE ALLOWANCE FOR EACH OTHER'S FAULTS, AND FORGIVE ANYONE WHO OFFENDS YOU. REMEMBER, THE LORD FORGAVE YOU, SO YOU MUST FORGIVE OTHERS".

So many times, people would ask me why I stayed if the situation I was in was as bad as it was. Even more than that, I asked myself. I never knew the answer, other than I kept hoping, and I kept forgiving. My relationship with Christ wasn't formed at that time, but I knew who Jesus was and I knew that I was supposed to forgive and not judge others. What I didn't know was that God never intended me to live in a beat up, broken life such as I was in. It is easy to get God's word misconstrued in our lives to fit the way we think it should, or the way others tell us we are supposed to interpret the word. But I am here to tell you that God's word is God's word. His word brings life, peace, joy and harmony. If it brings anything else, it is not of God. Forgiving Daniel for all that he did is in God's word, yes. But forgiveness does not mean that you have to continue to place yourself in the situation that brings you harm, hurt, and destruction. Do not confuse forgiveness with contentment like I did. We must always forgive those who bring us any form of hurt, whether physical, emotional, mental, verbal or sexual. But we forgive so that we may experience the freedom that comes with it. Remember, unforgiveness does no harm to those who offend you, it only brings harm to you taking you into a captivity that you do not deserve.

CHAPTER NINE
CONFRONTATIONS

Once I had found out that Daniel was talking to other women, he didn't even try to hide it from me anymore. In fact, he used the fact to degrade me further. He would leave to work telling me he was going to be late. I quit asking why because his response to me was that he had people to go and see. The worst was when he came home and still forced me to be with him. He would tell me during those times that the other girls were so much better, that they knew how to make him happy. He compared every part of my body to theirs and told me how much I lacked almost every day, He let me know that if I ever tried to leave that no one would ever want me. I completely believed him, after all, he didn't even want me, why would anyone else? Daniel would do something a little more every day that put more fear into me and lowered my self-esteem so deep I never thought I would want to look in another mirror again. It seemed the more he drank, the more his abuse escalated and the more he wanted to push the boundaries.

One night he told me to get ready because I was going to be going to work with him. He had been working security at an apartment complex, so I wasn't sure why I was going with him. I only knew I could not ask questions. Not without paying a price, and I had arrived at the point of trying to avoid as much abuse in any form that I could. I suffered in silence, but I thought that meant I had control of things. At least it made me feel that way. That night I saw just how rapidly things were escalating, and just how little control I had.

He drove around the apartment complex he was working security at and ended up parking, grabbing his binoculars, flashlight and telling me to follow closely behind him. I asked what he was doing, he told me we were going to watch a show. We walked around the complex stopping in front of a bush almost directly in front of a window that was someone's bedroom. I just looked at him and said we needed to leave. He ignored me. I started to walk off and he grabbed my hand telling me I wasn't going anywhere. I stood there shaking, looking around terrified. Before long there was a couple in that bedroom that began doing what couples do, undressing and making love. Daniel had his binoculars glued to his eyes and tried to get me to look, but thankfully didn't push when I refused since he was so into what he wanted to see.

That night was the first of many nights like this. I became his "lookout" since I refused to watch. He became so angry with me calling me names, as usual, and being forced to perform for him after he got out of "work" became more and more violent. The abuse I suffered escalated from verbal, to physical, and now the sexual abuse was to the point where the pain inflicted was more than I could handle. It seemed that no matter what he did, it was never enough. His drinking became worse, the abuse was out of control and I found out I was pregnant with my second baby. Just like before, I thought maybe this would be what settled him down, but unfortunately, he used it for his own desires and the cheating was worse than before.

I went for my prenatal appointment and was told I had a sexually transmitted disease called Chlamydia. I was so embarrassed. The doctor told me that Daniel would also need to be treated as well. When I told him, all he said was ok. I'm not sure what I was expecting, but it was as if he expected it. I was disgusted. But it did give me a break for a few days from him forcing himself on me. However, the more pregnant I became, the more hurtful things he found to ask me to do. I was having to pose for him, so he could take pictures in a manner that was very provocative, uncomfortable, and made me feel less than nothing.

By this time, Daniel was working a full time, as well as a part time job. He became friends with his part time boss, having him over often. As the days passed his boss began coming at times when Daniel was not home. It was during this time that I began to feel some worthiness again. Even though I was far along in my pregnancy, I was feeling beautiful once more.

Daniel never did find out, but somewhere in me I wanted him to see that someone did want me. I didn't have too much time to think about it though because his boss showed up at the house to tell me that Daniel had just been arrested and that we needed to go get the car from where it was and that he was going to go bail him out. I wanted to go to find out what he was arrested for because his boss wouldn't say, but Daniel had given strict orders to not take me to the jail. Well, when we went to get the car, imagine my confusion and shock to find out that our car was parked right behind my sister's apartment at her complex. At this time my family was not speaking to me, nor I to them, which happened numerous times in the years I was with Daniel. I could not understand what Daniel could have been doing there, and why was he parked behind her apartment instead of in her parking area which was in front of her place? I took the car home and had to wait for Daniel to get home so I could find out what had happened.

When he got home he told me that he had went to my sisters to talk to her and try to fix things between her and myself. He said my sisters husband had become angry because he said it was none of Daniel's business and they had ended up fighting, which resulted in Daniel being arrested, in which he said there were no charges because he did nothing wrong. However, I had an appointment and took a trip downtown to find out what exactly had happened. Since we were not legally married there was only so much information they would give me. They did tell me he was charged with disorderly conduct.

I called my sister so angry at her, protecting Daniel, defending him. Until I learned the truth. Daniel had been caught at my sisters prior to this day apparently and had been reported by tenants that he was looking into apartments. Having witnessed Daniel doing this, I knew it was true. On that day, he assumed my sister was alone because my brother-in-law had his car in the shop. Daniel was peeking through my sister's window and was greeted by my brother-in-law opening the door. Daniel tried to come up with a story, but he had already been caught looking in the window, so the two fought until the police showed up.

I confronted Daniel with this truth I found out, and he told me I could go with my family if I wanted to believe their lies but that they didn't want me so good luck. I sat there and cried. What could I do? No one wanted me. And now I had to continue living with someone who not only did all these horrible things, but he was now going after my family. Right when I thought it had become as bad as it was going to get, it always became worse.

The best blessing was my new baby boy. I would do anything and everything within my power to be the best mom to my children and protect them from what their father was. Daniel rarely interacted with the kids, he was so busy working, drinking, going out, doing security that by the time he came home it was so late. After each horrible thing he did, he knew just how to keep me hanging on.

He would come with a dozen roses, buy me jewelry, and later in the years he began taking us on trips. It was the "make-up" gifts that always gave me hope, and it was those same gifts that I learned to despise. I was still not allowed a house phone, or a car. I could use the car for appointments, but the mileage would be checked to ensure I went exactly where I was supposed to, nothing less or more.

I was still a prisoner, and it was only about to get worse.

PSALMS 34:17-18 NIV

WHEN THE RIGHTEOUS CRY FOR HELP, THE LORD HEARS AND DELIVERS THEM OUT OF ALL THEIR TROUBLES. THE LORD IS NEAR TO THE BROKENHEARTED AND SAVES THE CRUSHED IN SPIRIT.

So often I see and hear people who think Jesus can't do anything for them because they don't have a relationship with Christ. During my years in this, I didn't know God. I knew *of* God, but I had no clue how to pray, how to approach him, what he could do for me, or even what his word said, or his promises. But you see, that didn't make Jesus love me any less. And if you are in a situation where you think you have gone too far, you have done too much, or you just don't know how to get to where God is, let me reassure you that he knows how to get to where you are! The tears you cry, he catches them, the words you speak out in desperation, he hears them, the mess you find yourself in, he pulls you out of. There is only one name you need to know to get you started, it is the name of our Savior, our healer, our comforter, our redeemer, our restorer, the Messiah, it is Jesus!

CHAPTER TEN
HOSPITAL OR MY LIFE

Daniel decided after the incident with my sister that we needed to move away from where we were back to the small town where he grew up. I was so terrified that of being locked up in that trailer once again, but this time we moved into a house that one of his customers that he did business with on the side owned.

You see, Daniel was very charming, sweet, funny, smart…at least to everyone who wasn't family or myself. No one would believe how he was behind the scenes unless you really got to know him, and none of his customers did, so they all did side business with him.

The house we moved into was a big 3 bedroom, and for a normal family it may have been fixed up nice. I did the best I could to make it home for the kids, decorate with what I had, and took advantage of the times Daniel would "make-up" for his wrongs and buy angel items. Everywhere you looked in the house I had angels. I guess somehow, I felt protected by them.

We lived in this house for a couple of years in which many events happened during this time.

His older sister had married her high school sweetheart whom her dad had not approved of, and one of his younger sisters had become pregnant and her father had thrown her out of the house telling her to abort the baby. So, for a while we had both sisters living with us at separate times which seemed to help control the situation just a bit because there was no way Daniel could lock them inside the house as well.

He quickly grew tired of them being there saying I was having an affair with his brother-in-law. It had actually come to the point where anywhere we went, if I looked up I was having an affair with that person. I learned to walk with my head down to avoid conflict.

Since we had moved back to his small home town, Daniel grew close to his Uncle and Aunt that lived fairly close so most nights we were over at their place and Daniel was getting drunk. If we weren't there, then we were at yet another of his relative's home that ran a bar and he was getting drunk there.

I saw early on that Daniel was unable to control his drinking. I had been around my grandparents and mother who drank, but I had never experienced them as an angry drunk like Daniel was. Soon he became suicidal. I have to say there were times I thought that would be the only way I would ever escape. But I was always there to help him.

On most nights he refused to allow me to drive and would get the kids and I while he was heavily drunk and drive down the road at 180mph in our truck saying we were all going to die together. I also learned early on to talk smoothly and sweetly to him to calm him down when in reality I wanted to scream and knock him out. But I had my kids to think of.

There was a night that we were coming back from being at a dance out of town, his brother-in-law was driving at 75mph and Daniel opened the door and jumped. I half skidded, half held on until the truck stopped then ran to help Daniel who was unconscious. We never did call the police or ambulance, but how I wish we had. At least we hadn't until later in the years.

But this was my repayment.

Getting dressed as usual one day, after a few hours my leg began to itch, then I noticed bruising on the top of my thigh. Next thing I knew I was vomiting everywhere and couldn't walk. I asked Daniel for help and his response was that it was my problem, to deal with it because I needed to make dinner.

Two more days passed, and my entire left leg had swelled up, bruised, and I couldn't move it to save my life. My kids had spent the night at Daniel's parents and she came by that day to bring them back. She heard me in the room crying and went to check what was wrong. I showed her and told her I didn't know what it was. She told me I needed to get up because Daniel was going to get mad if I just laid around! I tried and fell.

She went to Daniel in the other room and began to tell him that I needed to go to the hospital, so I could get checked and find out what was wrong. He said no, that I just wanted to go to the hospital so that I could have all these men look at me and flirt with them. I remember quietly saying the words, please God. Whether I knew it would help or not I don't know, but at the time I needed something because I was getting worse with every passing minute.

His mother finally convinced him to take me to the hospital in the city closest which was only half an hour away. Once they saw what had happened they rushed me in saying I had been bit by a brown recluse. As they removed the poison the doctor told me had I waited one more day they would have had to amputate my leg. I was admitted, having to stay in the hospital for three months, learning to walk again with a walker, getting poison drained daily, which was so painful, and regaining strength again.

The nurses became my cheerleading team, I grew to know them well.

Daniel came by to visit me one time during those three months. I had to spend Thanksgiving in there alone. He didn't even come by that day.

The financial Aid advisor became my hospital angel. This man not only helped pay for the outrageous bill, he became my friend. The only friend I had.

He would eventually be the one who would help me, and my children escape to safety.

PSALM 139:1-4 NIV

YOU HAVE SEARCHED ME, LORD, AND YOU KNOW ME. YOU KNOW WHEN I SIT AND WHEN I RISE; YOU PERCEIVE MY THOUGHTS FROM AFAR. YOU DISCERN MY GOING OUT AND MY LYING DOWN; YOU ARE FAMILIAR WITH ALL MY WAYS. BEFORE A WORD IS ON MY TONGUE YOU, LORD, KNOW IT COMPLETELY.

There are things that happen in our lives that seem to be, "just at the right time". And there are times that "just the right person comes along". Well, these aren't coincidences, chance, luck of the draw. No, these are all God's timing. His plan set in motion. There is never a place, no matter how far we go, how dark our surrounding is, or how distant *we* may feel that God does not see us, know what we are doing, or have his hand setting things in motion for us. Yes, it would be great if we didn't have to walk through any trials at all, but Jesus tells us in his word that we will have trials, the thing we have to wrap our minds around is that *even during the midst of every trial* God knows and loves us! If you need rescuing, he is setting up the rescue team. If you need healing, he is setting up the doctors. If you need a word, he is setting up the intercessors. If you need restoring, he is setting up the rebuilders! If you have a need, the Lord has the plan already in motion! So, keep walking, do not camp out in the darkest of the dessert. Do not give up hope when your promise land could be just two more steps away.

CHAPTER ELEVEN
ATTEMPTED ESCAPE

Once I was released from the hospital I began to look at things differently. After being away from the daily verbal, physical, emotional and mental abuse for 3 months I felt almost alive again. In my mind I already had it all planned how I would get the kids and leave so we could have a normal life. I had the card of the financial advisor and he had told me of a place called women's protective service. In my mind it was all going to work out smoothly, and we would all finally be free.

Well, during my time in the hospital Daniel had his own plans brewing. If I thought his drinking had been bad before, I had not seen anything yet. He had begun to drink on a daily basis with his uncle and aunt and the entire situation had changed. It was not what I knew a relationship between nephew and aunt or uncle should be. I knew my family had a lot of issues as well, but what was happening was beyond dysfunctional.

I tried to keep things the way Daniel expected, so he wouldn't suspect that I was planning on leaving. But he was on vacation, so he was home all the time and I had no way to get to the closest city to where this protective shelter was, with him being home all the time. The only good thing that would come out of our going to their place every night was that Daniel would send me with his aunt to go to the convenience store to get food, so that allowed me the opportunity to be able to slowly save money without him realizing it.

After one of these nights, around midnight, Daniel decided that we were going to take a trip. He refused to let me drive or tell me what his intentions were for going. I was just thankful the kids were not with us at the time.

Once we made it to the city where he worked, he went to an apartment complex, told me to wait, got off and came back within five minutes. He did this at several different apartment complexes before we got to one where he took a while before coming back to the truck. When he did come back he had a handful of things and dumped it all on my lap and we took off.

I grabbed what he threw to see what it was and was in complete shock to see a lot of women's underclothes. I asked him who these belonged to, he told me they were in the laundry room and that is why people shouldn't leave things unattended. He told me not to be surprised, that it was where all the other stuff he had me try on was from as well. I told him that was stealing, that he was going to get caught and he slammed his brakes and placed his hand around my throat telling me they were mine now and I was going to wear them just for him.

Once we were home, that is exactly what he made me do. They were all so big on me. I was a small, skinny young woman because I never ate properly. Other than when I was in the hospital. For Daniel though, it didn't matter that they were big. He made me pose and do horrible things so that he could take pictures. He called his uncle and said we were headed back there. I tried to talk Daniel into staying home in every way I could think of even though it made me want to vomit. But he would not change his mind. Then I tried to see if I could stay home while he went, he again said no, saying that we had plans. For some reason I got chills all over and fear set in.

We showed back up at his uncles and he began drinking again. They were all so drunk and I just sat there feeling so out of place. And then the unthinkable happened. His aunt started dancing and taking off her clothes. Daniel went up to her and began dancing with her while she had nothing on, and his uncle was cheering them on! Daniel pushed me into his uncle who was in a disability scooter and told me to dance and take off my shirt. I refused. He called me a prude and told me if I didn't do it he would do it for me. I slowly started to mess with my shirt crying, trying to buy time. He began to walk over to me until he saw his aunt start dancing upside down on the sofa then all focus was there. I ran to the bathroom to vomit. I was sickened by the whole thing. I have no idea what all happened while I locked myself in the bathroom but when I came out the aunt was half dressed again and Daniel was on the sofa looking relaxed. We went home, he passed out and I began to gather bags for the kids. I knew I had to get out of there, and soon.

Daniel was home for another week before he went back to work, and that was when I knew it was time. One of his relatives and I had become close and she was the only one in his family who would acknowledge how he was and was willing to help me leave. While he was at work, she came over and helped me gather what I needed and took me & the kids to this woman's shelter where we could hopefully begin a new life.

The people in the shelter were nice. I had to tell them everything that was going on in my relationship with Daniel, which was hard to tell a stranger. The kids were having fun, playing and laughing more than I had seen in a long time. This place let me know that they would help me get a job, a house, an attorney, and everything else the kids and I needed to start a healthy life. No one was allowed to visit and calls out had to be monitored but could not be made for a few days. They had to ensure that Daniel would not cause trouble for the women there. We all had duties that were to be done daily, which was nothing compared to what I had to do when I was with Daniel.

It was Summer time, so I didn't have to worry about the kids going to school which was perfect. Since I had not been able to come with much they allowed us to get all the clothes we needed from a collection of stuff they had for women who went there for help. I heard some of the women's stories and it broke my heart. I couldn't believe I was one of those women now. I was only twenty-two years old and already had such a broken life. But I was determined to fix the broken pieces.

Daniel's family member that helped me leave came to visit as soon as I was allowed visitors. Her and I took both of our kids to the park, then to eat and afterwards she went with me to a house that I had found out through the shelter was for rent. The shelter informed me they would help me with rent until I was able to get on housing assistance and get a job to financially become independent. It felt so good to feel alive.

At this house, the owner was a wonderful elderly lady who herself had been abused at a young age and by the end of the house tour she told me she wanted me to buy the house and I could pay it in rental payments as I could afford. I was beyond shocked at what was happening. How could I be so lucky?

And then I received a call from his cousin the very next day. Daniel had tried to run my mother off the road and had been to my grandparents' house all night trying to get them to tell him where I was. I had not even talked to them in quite a while, but for some reason he assumed that is where I was going. He then let his cousin know if she ever saw me, to let me know that my family would be the ones to pay for me leaving until I went back. I felt hopeless, like I had no choice. The following day I called Daniel and had him pick me up and take me back. I paid that night for leaving him.

So back home, I was trapped, yet again.

2 CORINTHIANS 12:10 NIV

THAT IS WHY, FOR CHRIST'S SAKE, I DELIGHT IN WEAKNESS, IN INSULTS, IN HARDSHIPS, IN PERSECUTIONS, IN DIFFICULTIES. FOR WHEN I AM WEAK, THEN I AM STRONG.

Silent in tears we cry, we smile and inside we are falling apart. Why do we do that? During the time I was suffering in silence, I felt it was too much, more than I could take. But the truth is that there is never more than we can take! When Jesus came and lived life as we do, he suffered just as we suffer. He was betrayed, called many names, he was beaten, he was tempted, he starved, he was thirsty, he felt *all* that we feel. So it is then that we can stand proud in all the trials we face, during the darkest hours we face, we can truly smile and take comfort in knowing that we do not have to carry the weight of all we are facing because *Jesus already died on the cross for our hurts*! Once we can grasp a hold of this, we then can take hold of the power within each of us that lets us know the strength we have in Christ.

CHAPTER TWELVE

A WHIRLWIND OF PAIN

Because Daniel didn't trust anyone, not really knowing how I was able to leave, he decided we needed to move once again. I wasn't certain where we were going to be going, and honestly, by this time I really was having a hard time caring for anything other than caring for my kids and doing my best to protect them.

We ended up moving back once again to my home city. By this time, I had my third baby, my little boy. It was difficult because I was so close to my family but not able to talk to them. Throughout the time I was with Daniel I was able to talk with my family very rarely because he would get angry with them and decide I couldn't talk to them anymore. I wanted to share my kids with them but was only able to if Daniel said I could. I felt my kids were missing out so much on true family love.

The drinking never stopped, only became worse. But I did take comfort in the fact that we were far away from his uncle and aunt, so I was hoping that meant we would not be going there anymore. I was wrong about that.

One night after Daniel had friends over for drinking, he became very angry and began breaking beer bottles, and punching walls. His friends left saying they wanted nothing to do with it. I was begging them to not leave and stay to help me. I was in tears, but all they could say was they were sorry. The kids were asleep in their rooms already and all I could think of was to pray they would stay asleep. I had found myself praying a little more each and every day. It was all I could do anymore. I didn't know if my prayers were being heard, or if they would be answered, but I needed some kind of hope.

Daniel continued to break beer bottles calling himself the evil one, saying he was going to kill me. I was talking calmly to him trying to get him to calm down like I had in the past, even though I felt anything but calm. But this time it wasn't working, it was just making him angrier.

His fist was full of glass and bloody, I was making my way down the hall to make certain the kids were all asleep and were not about to come out, when Daniel ran to me, placed me against the wall broke a beer bottle right next to me, placing a sharp piece of the glass to my throat and made me tell him that he was the devil, that he was in charge of me, that I would never escape. I had to repeat everything he said. I stood right in front of the kids' room so that he would not be able to go in. No matter what I knew I would do whatever to protect them if I had to.

A few minutes later he broke down and began to cry, it was then that I was able to get him to the hospital. They did an immediate suicide evaluation on him and recommended that he be sent a state hospital for treatment. I was so relieved! It didn't last.

Daniel was admitted for two weeks and called me after the mandatory initial evaluation and told me I better get him out. I told him it was up to the doctors, he was angry and said I better figure it out. While he had been in there I was in touch with my family again. I was so scared, I called my sister and her and her husband took me to go and pick him up.

He did what he did best and convinced the doctors that he was completely sane, had no problems, and that his incident was a onetime thing, that he had never drank before. He was a skilled liar, that much was true.

Once back home, he went and bought me beautiful roses, a beautiful necklace, and took the kids and I on a trip. I had the smallest of hopes that this was finally the time he was going to change. But back home after he had me thinking that, we were back to the way things were before.

He had me ask my mother to watch the kids so that we could go on a trip for the weekend. I didn't want to because I knew anytime he wanted to take a trip alone it was never a good thing. I was right to be concerned.

We went out of town to a city a couple of hours away and checked into a hotel. He had me change clothes without anything under. I was shaking the entire time I did as I was told. We went driving around, it was already getting dark about this time. I will never forget the feeling of driving down the boulevard as he talked about what was going to happen, letting me know I had no choice. He stopped the car at several people walking the streets, these people that I knew to be prostitutes, came to the car offering their services. Even transvestites came with offers. I just looked down each time feeling sick to my stomach. He said no so many times, and I felt myself breath relief every time.

Then he went into a store to get something to drink and came out with a woman who was wearing almost nothing. He told me to scoot over and placed me in the middle. He told me we were about to have some fun. I was trapped.

On the way to the hotel he told her what he wanted her to do, to me. She began to do as she was told by him and all I could think was I want to die. He was very detailed about what he wanted, which let me know he had been thinking about this for a while already.

We went back to the hotel and he had her undress and began to tell her what he wanted her to do with, and to me. I said no and pushed the both of them away. I went to the corner of the room with nowhere else to go. Daniel was so into her that he didn't care that I didn't want to join, which I was thankful for but felt so bad for the woman.

He had her perform services for him. I just looked at him the entire time in disbelief. I remember thinking who was this man I was with? What in the world was I doing here and how did I end up here.

I have no idea how long we were there, it seemed like forever and at the same time it seemed as if it was only seconds. He pushed me in the back seat on the way to drop her back off, so that he could continue receiving services from her as he drove.

On the way back home, Daniel decided he wanted to go to his uncles and aunts, as if what had just happened wasn't enough, I was about to feel how much worse it could still get. My last thought that night, was God please help me.

PSALMS 51:1-4 NIV

HAVE MERCY ON ME, O GOD, BECAUSE OF YOUR UNFAILING LOVE. BECAUSE OF YOUR GREAT COMPASSION, BLOT OUT THE STAIN OF MY SINS. WASH ME CLEAN FROM MY GUILT. PURIFY ME FROM MY GUILT. PURIFY ME FROM MY SIN. FOR I RECOGNIZE MY REBELLION; IT HAUNTS ME DAY AND NIGHT. AGAINST YOU, AND YOU ALONE, I HAVE SINNED; I HAVE DONE WHAT IS EVIL IN YOUR SIGHT. YOU WILL BE PROVED RIGHT IN WHAT YOU SAY, AND YOUR JUDGEMENT AGAINST ME IS JUST.

We are so hard on ourselves. The enemy tries to keep us in the weight of sin, telling us that we have done what can never be forgiven in the sight of Christ. The lies that tell us our sin is too great, we have gone too far, we did too much, we strayed too far. But *lies* is exactly what they are. No matter what you have done, what has been done to you, what you were forced to do or chose to do. ***You are forgiven!*** When we believe the lies, when we convince ourselves there must be truth to them, what we are doing is crucifying Jesus all over again! He was already judged, and crucified for our sins and for the sins of others. Don't carry with you the shame of your past, or your present.

Jesus is telling you that you are forgiven, you are clean, washed, white as snow.

CHAPTER THIRTEEN
THE END OF THE DARKNESS

One of the last times I remember going to his uncle and aunts was a memory that would haunt me for years to come. Daniel had been drinking already, as was what I knew to be normal by now. When we arrived at his uncle's, it was close to eleven at night, I was already sleepy and just wanted to go home.

As soon as we got there I went to the living room so that I could try to sleep. I rarely said anything to either his aunt or uncle anymore since the time they had undressed and did who knows what else with Daniel. However, this time his cousins were there as well so there was loud music and nowhere for me to really rest. I did like the relatives that were there, the two were always so nice and treated me like a little sister. Although they had no clue how Daniel really was since they lived out of town they never saw much of anything. That was about to change though.

The party they were having had moved outside to the garage area, it was cold so most of us stayed inside the garage, except Daniel. I never really knew how Daniel was going to act every time he was drunk. He was an angry drunk, or a suicidal drunk. But he was always looking for trouble as a drunk.

Since I was in the garage with his family I didn't see what set Daniel off this time, all I knew was that his Uncle, Daniel and some other man were outside when I heard Daniel cussing at someone, then his uncle raised his voice. Although his uncle was in a handicap power chair, he demanded respect and for some reason Daniel always obliged with him, but never did anyone else.

We all went out there to find out what was going on and the most we could make out of it was that Daniel had taken something that was said personal and had become angry. His uncle yelled for him to go home and Daniel became a mix of angry and upset all at once. I happened to be standing against our pickup truck when Daniel lost his temper. It came on so fast that I had no time to react or move. I just stood there and prayed until I felt numb. My stomach took a beating that night, no matter what I tried, the impact was too much for me. I would find out years later that one incident would cause many problems with my digestive system.

I lost track of how many times he did this, I was honestly surprised I had not passed out, or maybe I had and didn't even know it. He finally grew tired and fell on the ground tired and crying. His aunt got him and took him inside to give him coffee and tried to sober him up and calm him down.

After not being able to move for who knows how long, his cousin came to help me move and walk me inside. As soon as I moved away from the truck, we both looked and behind where I had been, there was a big dent in the truck from the forceful impact of his attack. It had gone straight through me to the truck. Mind you, I was only 5'2 and weighed at most 90lbs at that time. I thought I would be okay, but I would find out years later that because of that incident, I would have to relive the nightmare.

I finally was able to get Daniel in the truck and take him home. I sat there watching him sleep with so many thoughts going through my mind. At one point, I went and grabbed his gun and just pointed it straight at him willing myself to just pull the trigger. He had threatened me many times that if I ever left again he would kill me with it. I stood there with the same gun he had used to intimidate me. I wanted nothing more than to just use the same weapon on him and end this once and for all. But I couldn't do it. Something inside of me told me to put it down. I would learn later that was the voice of God who I will always be thankful to for stopping me. I wouldn't kill him, but I would leave him. This time for good.

The next couple of days went by in a daze as all I could think about was how I was going to leave this time and never return. He did his usual trying to make up for things knowing I was in pain but not really remembering what he did. That was part of the problem, he never remembered what he did when he was so drunk, but I always remembered. I always had to live with the nightmare, I couldn't forget like he could. I went through the motions of thank you's and it's okay, allowing him to do what he always did.

When he went back to work, the same relative that had helped me leave to the woman's shelter, came over to visit and I told her I was leaving for good this time. She took me to her place, so I could make a phone call. I called the financial advisor that had been so nice while I was in the hospital and told him a little what had happened and what I was planning.

Within a couple of hours, he called back telling me the name of a hotel where I grew up that he had reserved for the kids and myself for a couple of weeks so that we could hide away. I was in tears so thankful for him and the help I was receiving.

Since I knew this was finally it, I told his cousin about a box Daniel had in the closet that I was never allowed to get near. Daniel used to put cameras in the house just to monitor what I was and wasn't doing. This day, I didn't care anymore.

His cousin helped me pull down the massive box, one because I was still in so much pain around my abdomen, and second because it was heavy. Holding my breath, I opened the box and I know my mouth must have just dropped open because his cousins was doing the same thing.

We turned the box upside down and threw all the contents on the bed. There were nude, and half nude pictures of women, young girls, of all sizes, colors, ages and positions. It was packed to the top with images. I picked up random ones and just couldn't believe all the women in these pictures. Some looked to be as old as their eighties, some as young as thirteen, possibly younger. I had no idea where or how, or even when he had collected all of these. It immediately let me know I had been living the past thirteen years with a stranger. I was ready to leave, and never look back. The time was now or never.

HABAKKUK 2:3 NIV

THIS VISION IS FOR A FUTURE TIME. IT DESCRIBES THE END, AND IT WILL BE FULLFILLED. IF IT SEEMS SLOW IN COMING, WAIT PATIENTLY, FOR IT WILL SURELY TAKE PLACE. IT WILL NOT BE DELAYED.

You and I. We were never meant to stay in a place of pain or heartache. We were never meant to stay in a place of abuse, whether physical, mental, emotional or verbal. Before we were even created in the womb, God breathed life into us. *Life*. We were all created with a plan and purpose in mind. It may seem at times like that plan will not happen, or the opportunity has already passed. I thought my time had passed when I went back after leaving Daniel the first time, but Jesus never turns his back on us. We are not a waste of time, we are not a nuisance to him. Keep believing, hold tight to those dreams, those desires, and those wants. No one can stop the plans of the Lord, no one. Remember that the next time you feel time is passing. He who has promised will see it come to pass.

EPILOGUE

I did leave for good that day. I stayed in a hotel paid for by the financial advisor whom later became a close companion. My children and I stayed in hiding until we were able to appear in court, in hopes that I would gain full custody of my children. Unfortunately, at that time in the late 1990's, it was still very hard to prove abuse. The Violence Against Women's Act signed by President Clinton was still so new and I was still so naïve to the law. I attempted to get a protective and a restraining order against Daniel, but both were denied. I had to get in front of court and tell the most private parts of the thirteen years, and Daniel told his side. The Judge sided with him and I had to share custody. He was granted full custody, with help from my own family, and I did not see the children for almost two years. But God promised I would get them back. He placed all the right people in my life along the way, and with their help, I was given my children back. Daniel decided it was not worth the hassle, because I would not go back with him. He still was granted rightful visitation, although it would eventually come to the point where Daniel would make less of an effort to be a part of the kids' lives, at times stopping completely.

I attended a school for adults and obtained my GED and was selected to do our graduation prayer. I also obtained my driver's license at the age of 27. I then went on to do volunteer work for a Christian agency so that I could gain working skills. I essentially had to learn to be an adult, while learning who I was. The kids and I were able to get an apartment and begin a life.

There were times I thought about calling Daniel. I fought to break free from what I knew. From comfort, even as painful as it was. The familiarity of being with Daniel was not easy to break. It never is when you are in an abusive situation. You are broken down piece by piece, degraded, until you feel lower than dirt, but somehow it is hard to get out of. But I am here to tell *you that you can get out*. I am not saying it will be easy, or that you won't have second, third, a million thoughts of returning. But I am telling you that if you remain strong in Christ, he will pull you through to the other side, the side known as the promise land. Remain strong in him and he will carry you in the darkest hours. He opened one door after another, and to this day continues to do so. He can and will do the same for you!

THIS BOOK IS DEDICATED TO MY THREE BEAUTIFUL CHILDREN, WHO GAVE
ME THE DAILY COURAGE TO KEEP FIGHTING FOR LIFE FOR THIRTEEN YEARS.
A SPECIAL THANK YOU TO MY HUSBAND WHO STOOD BY ME DAILY AS I TOOK
THE JOURNEY BACK TO WRITE THIS. AND TO FAMILY, AND FRIENDS FOR
BEING MY BIGGEST FANS EACH DAY I OVERCAME ANOTHER MOUNTAIN.
MOST OF ALL, THANK YOU LORD FOR WALKING ME THROUGH
THE WILDERNESS INTO THE PROMISE LAND!

ABOUT THE AUTHOR

Belle Lee began writing about her life, and the world around her, in the form of poems since she was very young. Her poetry has been published in World Poetry Movement where she was chosen as one of the best poets of 2012. The International Who's who in Poetry also selected her poem for publication in 2012. Having survived abandonment, abuse, rape, molestation among other life trials, has qualified her beyond what education could. She has true life experiences that she is ready to share with the world. Her current home is in Texas.

If you would like to share your Testimony, have questions, or want someone to pray for you, I would love to hear from you.

Belle72lee@gmail.com

Printed in the United States
By Bookmasters